This succinct book offers inspiration and motivation to continue searching, growing, and reconnecting to the authoritative sources of the spiritual life. I project that I am one of many, many others who will be brought closer to Our Lord by Hohman's examples of prayer and discernment. In particular, Hohman's straightforward tone and his ability to get to the essence of things will draw in many men who often seem to have a harder time exploring their relationship with God."

—**BETH SULLIVAN**, Executive Director, The Institute for Catholic Liberal Education

"I have had the privilege of being a small part of God's plan for the release of this book. As a believer it was thought provoking and solidified my need to understand and patiently await God's answer for my life in every situation. I would encourage anyone, believer or non-believer, to pick this book up. You will be pleasantly surprised by what you may learn and the difference it will make in your everyday approach to life's situations. A little inspiration no matter what the source may just be what you needed this very day."

—**JIM HINKLE**, Nuclear Engineer Cycle Manager

"When I began reading *Trust God*, I thought how much more can I trust God than I do now? What more can I do? How much more can I believe? Page after page, after page, pulled me in so deep. It was as if this book was written just for me, knowing my thoughts, hopes, fears, heart and soul.

"*Trust God* has allowed me to realize that all that I seek each and every day has always been with me = God. I just needed to stop looking elsewhere and trust!"

—**RICK VALENTE**, Operations Manager, Charitable Activist

Trust God

by Perry J. Hohman

ISBN 978-1-63393-883-0

Published by

 köehlerbooks™

210 60th Street
Virginia Beach, VA 23451
800–435–4811
www.koehlerbooks.com

TRUST
GOD

PERRY J. HOHMAN

VIRGINIA BEACH
CAPE CHARLES

TABLE OF CONTENTS

INTRODUCTION

Have you ever asked yourself if you are living life in such a manner that you would proudly present it to God today? Are you interacting with others the way God wants? Do you trust God to help you make daily decisions, and do you appreciate that God's responses are not always the ones you seek or on the timetable you want?

This book shares how to improve your daily life by becoming better at trusting God and identifying the creative ways and varied venues in which He responds to you. We live in a society that discourages reliance on God and instead fosters dependence on our technical devices that over time diminish our awareness of how God intervenes in our lives.

Each of your days is flooded with interactions with God. He's there! You just have to be better at opening your mind to His creativity. He communicates through others, written materials and with your conscience, particularly when you are quietly reflecting and seeking His input.

These writings capture various examples and means of how to trust God in everything you do, such as making decisions, helping others, strengthening your relationships, forgiving, assessing how you act with people and addressing strangers, just to name a few.

It is my hope that this book will help you perceive God's prompting and responses in your life, leading you to expand your trust in Him. Open your mind to God's vast reservoir of creativity, wisdom and patience. God's answers are not always the ones we want and they rarely arrive on our timetable. However, if you improve your trust in God and purposefully seek Him, your life will become more rewarding and peaceful, and one day you will happily and proudly offer it to God!

CHAPTER 1

START WITH GOD

Have you ever asked God to help you make a decision? Do you know He is listening? Do you know how to find His answers?

We all call on God's help in our moments of greatest stress. It is amazing how often we only seek assistance when the stakes are high. Sometimes it is easier to sense the hand of God when we need Him most, such as after we lose a loved one or are facing some catastrophic event. When life delivers such a crushing blow, our vulnerability leaves us more open to seek God's support. It is often during those times that we understand more clearly our vulnerability and limited role, and God's presence provides reassurance. We can rest in His embrace.

God answers us through many avenues. Part of the challenge of asking God for help is identifying His answers. We humans tend to look for specific answers to our dilemmas. Oftentimes, we don't recognize His responses because of our blindness, or we receive an answer that we don't really like. Or we see His answers as a coincidence, or just luck. We often take God's help for granted because things worked out so well. When you take the time to ask for God's input, shouldn't you also become better at recognizing His actual responses?

Learning to keep an open mind when seeking God's input will help you find the real responses to your requests. Often the answers to our prayers are not obvious because they unfold in sequences that require reflection and understanding. A lack of patience creates frustration. Allocating more time to reflect in prayer and encouraging yourself to be more patient will expand your awareness of God's responses. When I seek God's guidance, I try to become more alert to the interactions influencing my life and more attuned to how others intervene and engage me through events and conversations. I have found countless scenarios in which God inspired people at crucial points to take action, offer guidance or reassure me. When you become aware of God's interaction through your prayers and petitions, your outlook becomes more optimistic, knowing God is always with you.

A friend of mine once told me a story of his time in the military. He was new to the Navy and doing all he could to excel at his demanding career. He was keeping up his studies to advance his professional certifications while also working long hours, all during a time when his command was going through a massive overhaul. One morning as he arose for work, the whole thing snapped. His heart raced. He was sweating and felt short of breath. His body went into fight-or-flight mode and he took off. He rushed out of the room and jumped in his car. He gunned the engine and let the car take him a few blocks down the road. He parked the car and got out, holding his head, ready to let out a primal scream. Then he heard the bells . . . church bells. He paused and reflected on how God was communicating with him. The anxiety drained out of his body as he resolved that he could trust God and rest in the safety of the Lord. He returned to his post, strengthened.

I find myself continually seeking God's input at work, home and socially. Establishing and solidifying a foundation of trust helps me better cope with all outcomes, good or bad. The key to this partnership is to consistently circle back and identify God's input and actions.

Challenge yourself to view decision-making from God's perspective, and encourage yourself to select choices that align with His expectation of you. Visualize yourself discussing your options with God, and assess how you think He would respond. Say a prayer, ask for guidance and become more attentive to what's occurring around you. Many times, we miss God's direction because we are too focused on what we want, and His answers are not always the ones we seek or expect. Learning to keep an open mind and heart will help you find God's responses to your requests.

Oftentimes, we don't recognize His replies because of our pride, and we attribute God's answer to coincidence or just luck. Or the result pleased us so much that it distracted us from recognizing and appreciating God's input. Having a strong faith and a willingness to become more observant of God's interaction with your life will increase your reliance on and trust in Him, and improve how you respond to life's challenges.

Earnest, a good friend of mine, was on a mission where he and his family gave up everything they owned, including a successful business and a home, to live a life of trust in God. They traveled from place to place without resources, trusting God to provide along the way. Throughout their five-year journey, they continually prayed and sought God's help to provide them with food and shelter. As you can imagine, the trust needed for such a journey requires incredible faith, patience and an open mind. Their rewards, sacrifices and experiences have been awe-inspiring and a testament to how God responds to prayers.

On countless occasions, God interceded at desperate moments through unexpected calls from old acquaintances, and chance encounters with strangers. At times, the family was without food and resources, and they debated whether to go back to work in order to afford a meal. But in every instance, God miraculously intervened through unforeseen sources and means. On one occasion, Earnest had become so desperate to feed his family that he decided to interview for summer employment. He was offered the job and he figured it would generate about $2,400, enough to provide food and other needs for a number of months.

On the night before he had to give an answer to the prospective employer, he prayed to God for a sign: should he take this job and interrupt his mission? The next morning, Earnest received a phone call from a friend that he hadn't heard from in more than a year. His friend shared that he had just awakened from a dream in which he received a message to call Earnest and that he was to send $2,400. As you can imagine, Earnest was overwhelmed by his friend's generosity and God's intervention, which allowed Earnest and his family to continue their ministry without interruption. God's answers to your prayers may not always be as specific or dramatic as Earnest's, but learning to trust God to respond to your requests will noticeably improve your approach to life.

As you become more conscious of God's involvement in your life, uncertainty will become less of a concern. Since not all of God's responses will mirror your desires, increasing your trust will eliminate crippling fear about eventual problems. Sometimes God allows us to experience difficult events so that we will be prepared for something bigger. Instead of being overwhelmed by your bruised emotions, trust that God is preparing you for far more difficult scenarios that lie ahead.

Believe that disappointing results can be meant to prepare you. When you encounter such events, remind yourself that God has something far greater planned!

View your troubling situations as learning opportunities and you will prevent them from consuming you. The next time you find yourself in the middle of an unwanted situation, instead of becoming discouraged or looking to blame others, pause, say a prayer and thank God for helping prepare you for some unanticipated difficulty ahead. That's not easy. But remind yourself that demanding situations create the heat that forges your steel. As your relationship with God deepens, you will find yourself facing challenging encounters with a new vigor and stronger armor.

In a previous job, my employer decided to sell the company, which put my job in jeopardy. I had a young family and facing an uncertain future was extremely concerning. During my tenure at this company, I endured considerable stress, unrealistic demands and uncomfortable confrontations. These pressures intensified during the days leading up to the sale and thereafter. As the sale drew near, I prayerfully sought direction. I found myself waking up earlier in the morning, inspired to read the Bible. The more I read, the more I found peace. As long as I had my faith and my family, I knew God would lead me through this trial. I was prepared to lose everything I owned except God and my family. I continued praying and seeking direction.

Several weeks later, someone I hadn't spoken with in years called and informed me of an excellent and competitive job opportunity. I prayed over it and applied for the job. After several intense interviews, I was hired. My new job was in a dynamic and fast-paced environment with constant challenges and demands. As I found myself addressing issues daily, I realized that I would not have been adequately prepared to perform this job without my past experience in the previous pressure cooker. Today, I enjoy the job I have, which I've held for more than twenty years. The demands of the work haven't decreased, but I have realized that God allowed me to experience the uncomfortable environment at my previous employment in order to prepare me to address any new crisis with a calm and focused demeanor.

God's input in your life can be delivered in many forms, including friends, loved ones, a colleague, even a passing acquaintance. As your walk with the Lord deepens, you will more easily discern God's footprints on all of those unexpected suggestions that don't make sense at first. I have been humbled on numerous occasions when God spoke to me through children. Frequently, words spoken by my own children have caused me to slow down, revisit my thoughts and then make a more mature and morally responsible decision. Children keep it simple. Their perspective is motivated by wanting to please God, and their innocent questions often reflect God's interjection to confront our ambiguous decisions. When you show respect to a child, you become the moral teacher. When you listen to a child, they become yours.

Be aware that not everything you hear is good for you. The devil's work surrounds you as well, and he is clever and deceptive. Be on your guard as you weigh options. Be prayerful in making decisions. As your trust in God grows, you will become more proficient at distinguishing between good and evil. As you become more proficient at trusting God, living life will become more satisfying and rewarding.

What makes all of this easier? Repetition and self-assessment. Like exercise or other habitual routines, consistent daily use of your discernment and prayer muscles will help them grow. Find time daily to assess yourself. Review your interactions carefully, including how others might have interpreted what you did. Did your thoughts and actions cause harm to someone today? Were you open to the viewpoints of others? Of course you knew it was a joke, but did they? If both of you weren't laughing, then it wasn't funny. In fact, the joke may have been offensive. Evaluate your actions daily and seek constant improvement.

A wise priest, Father Bill from the Outer Banks in North Carolina, offered this practical message: Before your head hits the pillow, reflect on three events from the day. Identify something you did that day that improved the life of another person. Second, identify something you did that fell short of your goal to live faithfully. Pick apart specific conversations and interactions. Finally, prepare for tomorrow by asking God for patience and insight from today's experience.

Try to incorporate this personal review into your daily habits. Pick a good time every day for this meditation. Can you turn off the cell phone and radio as you make your commute home? Is there a chance to reflect before you sit down to dinner or watch your favorite television show? Can you squeeze in a few minutes before you go to bed? This daily exercise will make you stronger at facing troubles of the moment, and will contribute to an overall happier demeanor.

I find this quick and simple daily reflection vastly improves my outlook on life. It deepens my interactions with loved ones and colleagues and even helps me make better decisions in passing encounters.

Start with the good. Embrace positive actions. Were you inclusive and welcoming with others? Were you calm when tempers flared? Did you refrain from passing on that piece of juicy gossip? Did you plant seeds with others? Was your tone encouraging? Did you help a needy situation? Were your motives pure in that one encounter? Take a moment to note what you did well, and recognize God's involvement in your decisions and actions. Assess your role as a friend, colleague, spouse, parent, neighbor and, finally, steward of reconciliation. When you reflect on helping others, you reinforce these positive habits to your conscience, a feeling you will want to repeat.

When you fall short, note it. *Was I harsh in that comment? I could barely hide my contempt for that annoying person in our meeting. Maybe I should have called out my subordinate privately, instead of in front of the group. I was terse with that guy because he was being difficult. I'm too tired to complete that chore for my spouse.* Ask yourself how you could have better handled specific situations. Reflect on your own behavior, attitude and approach to others. Decipher the impact of your actions from the recipient's viewpoint. This may take some practice, but as we know, practice makes perfect! As you evaluate your day's actions through the lens of humility and sincerity, trust God to help with tomorrow's decisions. Then you will be better equipped to make decisions that are more pleasing to Him.

Bill, a friend of mine, always had difficulty with self-analysis. He drank too much and alienated his co-workers and loved ones with his salty verbal explosions. He returned to church to see if there was something he was missing.

His preacher's message was about reevaluating yourself using a simple inventory of each day's events. Bill admitted that this new routine was humbling and not fun. Yet, over time, he stuck with it and was able to see demonstrable improvement in his life. As he became less selfish and more forgiving, his life became more rewarding.

As you assess your actions, sometimes you may be required to apologize. As you spend more time in the daily habit of self-assessment, it will become easier to recognize when you have spun off track, so be prepared to combat your self-threatening pride. No need for "celebrity" apologies. The "If anyone was offended by my remarks" hedging in an apology will not serve you well. Arrange a call or quick meeting with the injured party. Be direct, swift and humble. "What I said was wrong..." "I was seriously out of line..." "I ask for your forgiveness..." Your lack of ambiguity will be the hallmark of your sincerity.

You will never have to apologize for a heartfelt apology. Outcomes from such encounters may not always be pleasant, but you will always be operating on the side of reconciliation, and your walk with God will deepen. Later, when your behavior in this incident comes up in conversation, you may not "look great" in the story, but you will be beautiful in God's eyes for how you handled it. When the words "I am sorry" come from your lips, the words "Trust in God" will be ringing in your mind.

DEEPEN YOUR TRUST IN GOD

- Allow God to steer you.
- God's answer may be different from what you seek.
- Embrace daily prayer.
- Assess your actions daily, quietly and alone.
- Be on the lookout for God's unlikely messengers, including children.
- Be wary of the devil's influence.

CHAPTER 2

PURPOSE THROUGH PRAYER

I mproving your prayer life is an integral part of living a more rewarding and faith-filled life. Praying is a conscious effort to seek God's help to live your life. You improve your prayer life by relying on and trusting in God. When you spend devoted time sincerely reflecting and meditating in prayer, your relationship with God intensifies and decisions are more manageable. When you make a heartfelt prayer, concentrate and allow your heart to be drawn more deeply into God's presence. Don't race through your words. Slow down, and understand what you seek.

When you stop making daily prayer a thing that you are "supposed" to do and just do it, your time management with God will improve. As I have matured in my spiritual walk, I have incorporated small prayers into more of my routine activities. These days, when I am performing mindless tasks, and we all have those, I have become more mindful of these moments as genuine prayer opportunities.

When I am brushing my teeth, I like to read an inspiring message from a prayer book or reflect on the needs of a friend or colleague who is in distress. When driving to work or traveling to fun activities on the weekend, I pray for guidance or direction into specific problems. At those times, I meditate on how to solve a situation, or even how to facilitate an upcoming difficult meeting. I pray for those who work with me, family members or anyone I know who is struggling. I ask God to place thoughts in my mind to help those in need of encouragement and to help me be His facilitator for real change. I ask for signs and try to become more observant of my interactions and surroundings. You will be pleasantly surprised by how a more reflective effort can overcome demanding challenges. Incorporate harvesting spiritual fruit in the same time and place where previously your mind just wandered. Now, that is time management!

I knew a businessman who had a frantic schedule filled with great responsibilities. His mornings were crazy busy and extremely stressful. A friend gave him some advice: "Try easing into your day with God." The businessman dismissed the suggestion as just one more task on the checklist, and continued having chaotic days that led to sleepless nights. One morning, after waking up early from a restless sleep, he began to think about his friend's recommendation. Instead of rushing ahead, he stopped and tried his best to talk through his upcoming day with God. Rather than a traditional prayer, his talk with God was much more like a brief listing of his goals for the day. It felt uncomfortable at first, but he kept at it. He talked to God while getting ready for work. Because he lived alone, he incorporated the ritual easily into his routine.

People began to notice changes in the man. His coping skills improved. Over time, he was better able to manage his tasks, and he came to enjoy strategizing business deals while chatting with the Lord, his new confidant, every morning. His demeanor with colleagues improved and his mind seemed sharper when he made big decisions. Talking is the first step to trusting God.

Other opportune times to inject prayer include when performing chores like mowing the lawn, gardening, shopping or doing laundry and cooking. I pray while I walk . . . throughout the day at work, around the house or in the neighborhood. These are opportunities to fit God into your busy life and keep Him central. Guidance, forgiveness, inspiration and insight all will become integrated into your daily routine, thus deepening your trust in God.

There are many forms of prayer. Some include reciting repetitive prayers that have existed for hundreds of years and which have wonderful meaning and lyrical wisdom. Other prayers can become specific requests and petitions of need. More prayers can be open-ended, soul-searching or even vague. When you pray, do you recite your prayers without focusing on the "meaning" of your words? Prayer requires concentration and sincerity. Be cognizant of what you are asking. Saying prayers without reflection and sincerity is merely an exercise in "checking the box."

Whether you recite traditional prayers or place yourself before God with your own petitions, become more attuned to your prayer requests. When reciting memorized prayers, slow down so that you hear in your mind the words you are speaking out loud. Since many of our memorized prayers are ones we learned as children, it is easy to gloss over the meaning or purpose of these sacred words. Pull out a written copy of the prayer so you can read each word carefully. If a prayer dates back to biblical times, envision what it must have been like for an individual facing those circumstances at that time. Embrace the intent of the words. Believe what you are asking. Visualize yourself in God's presence as He formulates His response.

You will often miss God's response if you are too focused on an anticipated outcome. When we focus narrowly on a specific result, we take away God's power to offer a creative reply. There is nothing wrong with asking for specifics, but don't allow yourself to obsess about a particular outcome or timeline. When you "lock on" to expected results, you prevent yourself from discerning God's true desire. Waiting for a certain outcome implies that you believe your own ideas are best. Perhaps God has something else in mind.

I remember one Sunday when my son and I prepared meals for the poor. We knew this one place where thirty or more homeless people normally gathered. We were surprised when only one man showed up that day. I said a prayer and asked God why there were not more people and what could we do. Suddenly, the one guy we were feeding asked if we could take a drive five miles down the road where he knew of a woman and her four kids living at a campsite. We immediately headed for our adventure. We missed a couple of turns but eventually found the campsite and we saw the mother come out of her tent. Noticing that she was apprehensive, we assured her we just brought meals at the suggestion of someone who knew her situation. She began to weep intensely, which sent shivers down my back. She shared how she had run out of food the night before and was concerned for her children. Normally, we feed thirty people on that day, but this time we fed only six, which felt like a crowd. As I said a prayer of thanks to God for leading us to her, I also realized that God's outcomes may not be what we request or expect. Remind yourself of that when you make your next prayer request!

God operates through many avenues, including children, new people in your life, books, articles, programs and Scripture. Countless times, my children have asked me about someone who has drifted from my immediate circle. Without exception, when I call that person, I find them facing a huge struggle and my call is a real help. That is God speaking to me through the actions of children. I now routinely ask God in prayer whom I might help, then clear my mind for a name to pop up. These suggestions are often game-changers. A business acquaintance told me the story of seeing just one too many men with their hands outstretched at a stoplight when he murmured something about "that bum getting a job."

His young daughter reminded him that his favorite phrase to say was "We are all God's children." "That makes him your brother, right?"

she asked. His daughter was the catalyst for softening his own heart. God's change agents can come from any corner of your life. Make a habit to notice more.

Ten years ago, Marie, a relative of mine, met Leroy, a Vietnam vet. Marie was an alcoholic and Leroy had a nasty cocaine addiction. Their lives were filled with temptation and failure, bordering on complete collapse. The two became desperate one day and prayed to God for help. The next day, a relative of Leroy's called and invited them to church. During the church service, they both felt the power of the Holy Spirit.

After that, Marie and Leroy began to seek genuine change in their lives. They relocated immediately, leaving behind dangerous acquaintances and a rotten environment. Two weeks later, they were settled in a new community where they helped to launch a ministry serving meals to the homeless. They took direct actions to eliminate their addictions and concentrated on serving others. They got married and cleaned up their lives. Today, Marie and Leroy are celebrating their tenth anniversary running a weekly food kitchen that serves more than 200 people a week. Their efforts would have failed if they had acted alone. But they were assisted by a mighty and forgiving God whom they now praise in word and deed. They have never been happier.

Prayer is a conscious effort to ask for God's participation in your life. As you become a better communicator with God, you will notice God's larger role in your affairs. God will provide more guidance, direction and inspiration in your life. You just have to seek and become better at recognizing His responses. When you do, your reactions to situations will become more gratifying and you will experience a satisfying inner peace as you realize God's hand is firmly in yours. You will witness how God places certain individuals in your life at crucial moments to address challenges or achieve unexpected success.

I recall a time when a holly tree in our yard fell, taking out our new neighbor's fence. Jacob and Terri had just moved into their house, which was in an adjoining neighborhood but still backed up to our property. It made no sense that a 100-foot-tall tree could just fall over, doing damage to both properties. I was not feeling blessed at all recognizing the financial hassles ahead. A few nights later one of their guests heard a loud noise at 3 a.m. He looked out the window and through the hole in the fence could see that our garage had caught fire. Because of the broken fence, Jacob was able to race over to our house in seconds, bang on the door and yell "Fire!" My wife, Theresa, and I called 911 and evacuated our kids and their friend who was spending the night. Jacob did his best to slow the fire with a garden hose. By the time firemen were on the scene with their hoses pressurized, the garage was ablaze and the main house at risk. The firemen quickly put out the fire and our dramatic moment passed.

Upon reflection, I understood how blessed we were. Our previous hassles prevented the worst outcome. If that holly tree had remained standing it would have completely blocked Jacob's view of our garage, and the new shortcut through the fence provided by my fallen tree saved Jacob five valuable minutes getting to me.

These may be just coincidences that can be easily explained away, but when such things happen to you and you rely solely on God, they take on a deeper meaning. God intricately weaves events and individuals into our lives, and the more active we are in prayer, the more likely we are to see His fingerprints. Be more observant. God's responses to your life are there when you look.

As you experience God's responses to your prayers, thank Him. Go overboard. I believe God smiles when He hears a sincere *thank you*. I can't imagine that He tires of hearing them. I wonder if we disappoint Him when we fail to thank Him for our ongoing blessings. When you accept God's responses in your life, you replace fear and uncertainty with confidence and deep peace. Pray more and learn to communicate with God. He is listening and responds!

DEEPEN YOUR TRUST IN GOD

- Your relationship with God intensifies with prayer.
- Recite memorized prayers out loud and grasp their meaning.
- Ease into your day with God.
- God's outcome may not always be what you sought.
- God communicates through children, co-workers and others.
- God answers prayer. Be more cognizant of how to hear Him.

CHAPTER 3

ELEVATING RELATIONSHIPS

A s we live our lives, we surround ourselves with the individuals we love and trust the most. These are the people we enjoy during our memorable moments, and rely on during demanding challenges. They are family members and friends, people you love the most. They need to know that. Do you frequently communicate the importance of your relationships to those you hold most dear? If you can't remember the last time you told them, then it's been too infrequent.

You must protect and fortify your most treasured relationships. Time is your greatest resource here. Devote more time to expressing your appreciation for those who see you up close. Some of the easiest fixes in a marriage involve spending more time together. When you share experiences without distractions, your focus deepens, empathy returns and joy increases. The electronic devices of today need to be stowed away in order to enrich your other connections. Keep one device up and running—your ears. When you listen, your heart responds.

I am a fan of capturing magic moments, those frequently spontaneous gestures of glory with my relationships. I recall many special moments with my wife, children and friends. They include heartfelt toasts, warm embraces and sincere and loving words shared, particularly with someone in need. Our family and friends like to gather together, tell stories, kid around and have quality time together. Invariably, one of us will remark, "We're having a moment!"

I recall such an episode at my daughter's wedding, right before my wife and I walked her down the aisle. We three gathered in a hug, looked each other in the eyes and shared our most personal expressions of love. It was a deeply serious and profound experience, but we all laughed when my daughter closed with "We're having a moment." Events like that are some of my favorite captured moments. I recall them often because they are so joyous to me. I also frequently bring them up with loved ones, reminding them of these anchors of pure joy in our time together. Recalling your treasured experiences often can strengthen your relationships. Reflecting on pleasant moments and asking God's blessing will make you more appreciative and forgiving of your loved ones. Finish your special moments by sincerely asking God to bless one another and thank Him for providing such reliable and loving friendships.

Fortifying your most treasured relationships requires spending more time, thought and energy to improve them. Do not let devices and toys substitute for direct contact. Plan more family and friendship meals without devices at the table. Clear away disruptions and speak only of positive, uplifting topics. Focus on what is fun about your spouse and kids. Don't let trivial matters interrupt you. Steer the conversation to positive, uplifting topics, putting the downers aside. Your loved ones will emerge from their silos and open up to engaging hospitality.

Consider meeting at places away from your daily environment to avoid regurgitating mundane daily recaps. Take a walk in your neighborhood, along the beach, a lake or trail, or just sit in your backyard. The change of scenery can be the catalyst for the change of communication. Keep the topics uplifting. Stifle your inner judge. Emphasize your utter devotion to and appreciation for the other person. Set your eye on the horizon.

If you have difficulty expressing your love and devotion, ask yourself "Why?" Are you too wrapped up in your own needs? Are you hanging on to a piece of old news that you can't seem to let go? Is there some recent infraction that you feel has not been adequately addressed? Let those go. Not forever, but for now, for this moment. It can wait. Remember, you are trying to build a foundation of magical moments which can't flourish in soil saturated with recrimination.

Your responsibility to children only deepens your obligation to devote the resources of your heart and mind to others. Kids want your time more than anything else you can offer. They yearn for your involvement in their lives. They want you to deliver the straight scoop on success, failure, hardship, lordship, devotion and the other complexities of love that you have learned, evidenced by one raw scar after another. Kids see everything we hope to hide because they are usually seated behind us. Even with such insider knowledge, they look to us for the influence and spark that will help guide them through every difficult decision.

When I was in high school, my parents made me attend a spiritual retreat. I went reluctantly. At one point during the weekend, letters were given to attendees written by people who knew them. The letters I received were powerful and spoke about individuals who were praying for me and even enduring small sacrifices to keep my retreat top of mind. These sacrifices had a name. They were called *palancas*. A palanca is a disruption of a routine which reminds one person to think about another person. I was really touched by how many people were actively participating in my retreat, even though they were at home. The letters gave details of where and when people planned to pray and sacrifice for me. I started to adopt the practice of palanca in my life. It created one of my most profound moments with my dad.

When I was twenty-eight, my father was diagnosed with pancreatic cancer and was given six months to live. I chose to carry a stone in my shoe to constantly remind myself of my father and his painful journey. I wrote him a letter sharing how I felt our relationship was like a rock: everlasting. I told him that I appreciated how he raised me with inspiring messages, discipline, a strong work ethic and compassion. I told him about the rock in my shoe and how it had been a help in reminding me of his arduous fight with cancer. It was a deeply felt letter, and I admit I was a little hurt when I received no reply.

Months later, as Dad was nearing the end, I went to see my father. We took a long car ride and when we parked, I took off my shoe and handed him the stone. I told him how hard I had been praying for him and the stone just kept reminding me that I needed to do more. He recalled how much basketball I had recently played and wondered whether I had worn the stone through all that. I assured him that I had, but that pain was nothing compared to what I knew he was facing each day. He said he had forgotten my original letter because of all that was going on when he received it, but now it was coming back to him. He was overwhelmed with emotion and he wept – it was the first time I saw my Marine Corps and CEO father cry. We shared a hug and did not break the silence. I understood the power of palanca from that point on. Embrace your own palanca sacrifices to bless your most treasured loved ones. You won't regret it, and your heart will be rewarded.

If you placed a rock in your shoe to witness to all the important people in your life, you would have to buy larger shoes. Many of your daily interactions with people will not be highly emotional, deep encounters, and you will not be called upon to offer genuine witness. Still, these secular encounters are a reflection of your spirit, and they supply evidence to others, including strangers, that your faith is active. Are you addressing and respecting others in the same manner as you would approach God? That's a high bar but it should be on your mind. The starting point is simple: appreciation. Make a habit of expressing appreciation. Expressing thanks for the efforts of another, even if the results are not fully what you expected, shows that you are aware and care enough to comment. It is a simple, infectious gesture of goodwill. Do not take the time and services of others for granted. People will wonder what is inside a person who is so attentive to small graces. You become a witness to God's love without preaching or quoting scripture.

My friend John, a businessman, did something on a business trip that caught my eye. We stopped for breakfast and after we placed our orders, the lady at the counter asked if we needed anything else. John looked around and spotted a stranger sitting alone. "Add whatever that man is ordering to our bill," John said. The man appeared initially uncomfortable with the offer, but John insisted and the man happily ordered. John and the man exchanged pleasantries and you could see that everyone in the room appreciated the "pay-it-forward" gesture. When we drove off, I asked him about what he had done. John got a thrill from providing such generosity to strangers because it always caught them off guard, and he felt that you could set the tone of the whole day for another person with such a simple act. He knew his actions would motivate the man, and others, to offer someone else a break in their own unique way, inspired by seeing such a simple gesture. The falling dominoes are thus set in motion. John's out looking for his next "victim."

As with strangers, we must keep the same positive attitude with co-workers. Be a force for good in your workplace. Teamwork creates unity, which is necessary to achieve complex business goals. The workplace may be a particularly troubling area of your life for making plans for devoted witness. You may be under great financial pressure with your job, or you may be reporting to someone who has lost your respect by behaving badly. There is very little under your control in a work environment, particularly one that is changing with market and product needs. Work has stress at every level. The pressures from above can be excruciating, and you will always be expected to pivot and change as needed for the greater good of the organization. Your individuality may not be cherished in the workplace, and the decisions that heap more stress on you are often made by others. But you can always make a positive difference.

One of our most influential employees is our receptionist, Kathy. She is an uncompromising egalitarian. Everybody who walks through that door gets a huge smile and her undivided attention while they are guided to the proper person. Kathy's phone manners are upbeat, earnest and helpful. People know that she is interested in their business and they see her as a resource. Some of the unpleasant and tedious tasks of the office are her responsibility, but she handles the workload with a good cheer that is surprising under those circumstances. She displays respect and optimism, frequently changing the dynamics in a meeting. Her demeanor is a key reason for the positive attitude of many who walk through our doors.

We make better decisions as a team due to her actions, yet she is responsible for very few of those decisions. Customers trust her and come to trust us. She is an ambassador for her faith without ever needing to mention it.

Every person in an organization can improve the company's performance through their own conduct. If you are the boss, you must be acutely aware of this. You should live properly within the corporate culture and rules that you have set for others to follow. Be encouraging, patient and approachable. Being cognizant of a subordinate's difficult personal situation may help you defuse a crisis when the employee is unable to perform as needed. Offer correction in the calmest tone possible. You must be observant and encouraging . . . the approachable coach. Your optimistic mindset drives morale.

For the vast bulk of us somewhere in the middle of the employee ranks, strategies also exist. Humor is a good tool to keep discouraged individuals motivated. A good chuckle can cut through a tense moment and relieve stress in uneasy colleagues. Keep the laughs appropriate and not directed at any individual. When the jokes run dry, simply share a friendly smile. Demanding people and stressful situations are the norm for many work environments. Fight back with a happy demeanor.

Assess your work environment and determine if it is the right fit for you. Seek a position that meets your interests and your monetary requirements. Sometimes, in today's economy, a lesser position or a lower wage may be the only option. How do you avoid being discouraged? Consider the possibility that this current position might be preparing you for something more promising. You may encounter an influential person while performing your current assignment, and your work will be noticed. Witnessing your approach to the easier tasks may show how you take responsibility for even the smallest detail. Have the resolve to maintain your positive attitude and trust God to guide you with all your work responsibilities.

If you are not receiving satisfactory or complimentary feedback from your boss, be realistic in your self-assessment. Consider whether you should pursue a position that is more commensurate with your talents. Several of my fellow employees have sought my counsel to assess whether a new position was the right fit. Almost every time, the individual was quite relieved to discuss their discomforts with their current job. Often colleagues are in way over their heads, engulfed in stress and uncertainty, or too prideful to reach out for help. Many can fix the problems with their current job, but some must make a change. Should you seek a position more tailored to your talents? Finding a job where your skills are more appreciated will provide you with satisfaction and eventual success.

Ultimately, the skills you acquire by improving your most intimate relationships will be helpful in your encounters with others. When God is allowed to be an active participant in your relationships, they will strengthen. His presence will protect, nurture and deepen your bond with others. Those at home and in your social circle will see your fresh, optimistic approach and reciprocate. Work, home and social relationships become more fulfilling when you trust God to guide you in your daily decisions, encounters and relationships. Constantly ask God to bless and nurture your relationships.

DEEPEN YOUR TRUST IN GOD

- Capture your magic moments with your spouse and loved ones.
- Kids need your time, so give them plenty of it.
- Shower your spouse with approval.
- Improve your work environment by reaching out to co-workers.
- Be the undimmed light at work.
- Use clean humor to defuse tension.

CHAPTER 4

MAKE A DIFFERENCE

Have you ever spent time meditating on what God has called you to do? Try it. Spend some prolonged time quietly, alone in a restful place without electronics or other distractions. I find enjoying God's natural works of beauty improves my focus, like sitting by the ocean or a quiet creek. Let the stillness calm your heart. Saturate yourself in God's natural beauty and ask Him to flood your mind with His intentions. Engage God! Seek His desires for you.

Don't miss God's missions for you. There was a prominent couple in our community who had great kids. All seemed fine. The wife began hanging around recently divorced women and started hiring babysitters for "girls' night out" events. She eventually asked for a divorce, moved out of her home and lost custody of her children. Her former husband eventually remarried and built a future with his new family. Later, when the former wife reflected on her behavior, she admitted that the immediate pleasures of a freer lifestyle felt pretty awesome. That euphoria made it easier to lose track of her happily married friends and run with a more disaffected crowd. She regretted being blind to her mission as a wife and mother, damaging so many lives and failing to be the right role model for the children she loved.

Don't expect a Hollywood moment when God reveals Himself to you. I heard about a surfer who was caught unexpectedly in a violent ocean storm. His predicament required his rescue a few hours later. It was the most frightening experience of his life. A friend asked if he had prayed to God for help. The surfer said he always doubted the existence of God, so asking for His help did not feel right. Maybe, his subtle friend suggested, the surfer's discomfort with asking God's help proved, deep down, that he believes He exists. This conversation inspired the surfer, who now seeks God and talks to Him when he surfs. That's a Hollywood moment.

God is always calling you to help in some way. Opportunities arise every day to improve the lives of those around you. You just need to be courageous enough to act. God is God, both creator and creative, so pay close attention to the thoughts He places in your mind and the people He places in your path. Several events may happen before you recognize how God is guiding you. Your mission may be unfolding before you, but sometimes you have to slow down to see it.

I never would have written this book without God's inspiration. I am very comfortable asking God in my prayers what He wants of me, and writing a book was surely the last thing on my list! I am not a writer. I am not a theologian. I know people who can quote Scripture from memory and others who give powerful sermons. A number of years ago, I was helping to hold together a business in a demanding economic downturn while supporting a wonderful family. There was little spare time. Yet, God woke me up from a sound sleep one night, bathed me in the warmest sense of peace, and filled my mind with the inspiration to write this book.

I spent the next few weeks trying to convince God this was a dreadful idea because I had huge doubts about my ability to add another impossible task to my daily routine. I normally don't bargain with God, but this seemed like a task too far. So I finally prayed that if

He really wanted me to do it, I needed some sort of sign. A few nights later, the title of the book came to me in a dream. So I got busy writing!

Over the course of ten years, I have sought the Holy Spirit's guidance before the start of each writing session. I prayed for God to fill my mind with a topic and provide me with the thoughts He wanted me to share. The Holy Spirit allowed words and concepts to pour forth. I was the conduit. If there is fruit in this writing, God produced it. If any of these words touch your heart, it's because He deems it fit.

The point here is to encourage you to start pursuing God's mission for yourself, today. All of us have something to offer that can benefit our neighbors next door and around the globe. God invested talents in you and they have a purpose. One day you will answer for how you used those gifts. Avoid arriving at God's house with little or no results. Ideas for missions include: feeding others, literacy training, delivering meals or supplies, house repairs and good old-fashioned listening. Not sure where to start? Research charities or religious institutions that appeal to your interests. Don't be surprised if you are led into unfamiliar territory with new faces and fresh demands on your skills.

We all have the ability to fill a need and improve another person's life. You are not the exception to that rule, no matter how powerful your insecurities. God does not make useless beings. Your talent will emerge. Don't allow fear of failure or the opinions of others to discourage you from initiating an action. If the devil can intimidate you to doubt yourself, you will remain a spectator on the sidelines. When you share your time, skills or financial resources, you are providing a meaningful return on God's investment in you.

If you are a person of means, donating funds is crucial. When you give financial resources, you know that many individuals will receive support that would not have been available without your generosity. My friend, an executive director of a leading charity, encourages me to visualize the outcome of a donation. Whether it is providing meals, clothes, education or housing, I say a prayer and visualize the beneficiary. Even when I am feeling a financial pinch,

I reflect on the fact that there are many people in the world much less fortunate than I am, and my resources can be spread to many through a carefully selected charity or religious mission.

When you donate your time, it deepens your connection to the challenging circumstances others endure. My family and I have enjoyed serving breakfast to the homeless for several years. Rarely did we ever walk away without one of us experiencing a profound encounter. Countless times, just engaging someone in a conversation lifts their energy and improves their outlook. People notice when a stranger expresses sincere concern for their troubles. I pray that the recipient sees God's love in our exchange. Volunteers are merely the instrument of His work.

Many years ago, when I was first inspired to serve meals to those in need, I gathered breakfast and went searching for hungry people. I was hoping to have an impact by reaching large groups of people, but I found only a couple of small clusters. Then I asked God to lead me. As I turned a corner, a man was struggling on his bicycle, so I asked him if he wanted food. With a big smile, he accepted my offer and thanked me. I asked if he knew of more people in the area. He pointed behind me to show the way to a nearby shelter. When I turned back around to thank him, he was gone, and just like that, there was no one around for blocks. God must have sent me a messenger. The encounter created an indescribable sense of euphoria within me. I still think of my "mystical moment" when I serve at a soup kitchen.

The gift of your time can be multiplied by involving young children. When young people witness challenges outside their comfort zone, it expands their horizon and deepens their empathy. I remember a time when my eight-year-old daughter and I had a conversation with Mary, who was living on the streets. We spoke for almost an hour and when we were finished, Mary looked us in the eyes and thanked us. Then she asked God to bless us. To this day, my daughter still mentions Mary. Mary lit a fire under both of us, and her memory lives on in our fulfilling joy of philanthropy.

Trust God to lead you in your missions. Ask Him to identify your next missions and keep your talents sharp for service. As you encounter your new assignments, enjoy the centrality of God in your life as you witness others being helped by your actions. Envision the day you meet God and how inspired you will feel at His satisfied smile. He recognizes the fruits grown from the seeds He gave you to cultivate. Plant as many as you can, and be a positive difference maker in your surroundings!

DEEPEN YOUR TRUST IN GOD

- Reflect on what God has called you to do.
- Be open to guidance from the Holy Spirit.
- One day you will be held to account for how you used your talents.
- Helping others is your life's mission.
- Plant, cultivate, harvest, share.
- Inspire others to join you.

CHAPTER 5

PACE YOURSELF

Thereare many activities available in your life to absorb your
spare time, whether it's enjoying your hobbies, fulfilling family
obligations or engaging in some form of entertainment. But
excessive time spent in one pursuit can evolve into an addiction.
Addictions are not just related to drugs and alcohol. Addictions
can include working too much, excessive social media, sports
and entertainment obsessions, gambling or reading inappropriate
material. Addictions are time thieves and can be easily substituted for
the necessary moments of uninterrupted fellowship with God. If you
sometimes wonder why you do not feel close to God, do an inventory
of your addictions.

Are you spending your time wisely on this earth? At some point
God plans to ask you this question and it might be prudent to be
thinking of a reply. Certain activities are necessary for survival, such
as eating and sleeping. Most of us allocate a significant amount of our
time working for a paycheck that provides food, shelter, clothing and
other essentials. What we do and what we earn can say a lot about
us. Yet, how we spend the remainder of our time often molds our
character. It is healthy to assess your time management periodically,

which can often reveal glimpses into your subtle addictions. Recognize that the devil is behind all addictions, those powerful, concentrated temptations that are detrimental to our better selves.

Evaluating your time management can take on a spiritual dimension when you consider that addictions can drain your remaining time on this earth by constantly demanding that you "feed the habit." Life is not fun if you are a slave to addictions and their ramifications. *Groundhog Day* is a movie many enjoy, but addiction gives you the repetition depicted in the movie without the laughs or Bill Murray. The thing that you think is probably okay in your life, all things considered, may be what God wants you to trim way back if it is absorbing a significant amount of your time. He is eager to offer you a meaningful alternative to what you don't even realize you're handcuffed to. He even offers a few easy first steps.

Spend more time in communion with Him. He's flexible. There are lots of ways, but God especially favors a few of them. For starters, there is the Bible. The Bible is an inspiring library of books from God with answers to many of your questions. Unfortunately, many people are needlessly intimidated by it. Sometimes the language in certain translations confuses people and they get lost in it. Or maybe you might feel some slight embarrassment if someone caught wind of you reading Scripture as if you were some sort of religious fanatic. But if you want to get on God's team, you have to take a look at the playbook.

Read the Bible every day. Push yourself to just do it . . . maybe in the morning or maybe at night, or maybe both. God wants that. Praying is emphasized throughout the Bible and by the Prophets. God is also crystal clear on this one. I use my morning prayers and my evening prayers for slightly different things. My evening prayers are reflective and may linger on an experience from the day. My morning prayers are usually motivated by a biblical passage I have read, and they center on ways I can be productive and spiritually mindful that day.

If you already make time in your day for Scripture reading and daily prayer, congratulations. Keep it up! Envision God smiling at your commitment and saying, "Nicely done." Amplify your awareness of His growing presence in your life. From a time management perspective, you will have dedicated chunks of time to fortify your spiritual development well outside of work and family hours.

God also wants you to be in fellowship with others. Maybe that is difficult to do every day, but choose to be a regular participant at your house of worship. Consider joining a committee or making yourself available for some weekly or monthly function. Look for something that suits you so that it's rewarding and doesn't feel like a chore. God wants and needs you as His conduit to encourage other fellow believers to profess His goodness and love for us. He knows what is good for you and can lift you up. Sometimes it can be tough to stand up and own your faith while people are snickering or sneering about something you hold dear. But God knows you need support and He is always there for you.

God wants you to help others, particularly those in need. Is there a cause or charity that could use your gifted skill sets? If you personally were given a whole week to devote to a single cause, what would you choose? Two of our kids had the honor of spending time on a mission trip with Operation Smile, a wonderful organization dedicated to worldwide cleft-palate correction surgeries. Language was a barrier in the remote villages where they worked, and it was part of their job to comfort the nervous parents before their children's surgery. All they could offer these worried parents were calming words, eye contact, holding hands and prayer. My kids spoke of the presence of God as these families were transformed from nervous to elated at the return of their vulnerable children, sporting an intact smile for the first time in their lives. The blessing was not only shared by the surgery recipients but also by volunteers experiencing a joyful heart.

What organization, including your place of worship, marries your passion with your sense of justice and human dignity? Find it and give them a call. Offer up a day or a weekend or whatever amount of time makes sense. Since you are deeply moved by what they do, you are more likely to repeat your actions, reaping the joy that comes from making a difference in the lives of others.

The bottom line is simple. Let your life's actions reflect your intentions. Identify where the majority of your time is spent and determine if it is preventing you from being a better person to your family, neighbors and God. As you examine your use of time, determine how many hours you spend helping others or learning about God. If that number is low, chances are you have at least one addiction.

If you want to see God one day, then commit more of your time to Him. It will never be more complicated than that. Refrain from watching too much television, consuming social media, playing computer games and other distractions, particularly when inappropriate messages and images dominate those activities. Allocate more of your time to interacting with loved ones and those in need. Spend more quiet time alone meditating on God and asking for His direction. If you sincerely ask God for proper guidance, He will provide it. Remind yourself that God's responses may not fit your timetable and may not always be the ones that you're looking for, but God will never ignore you! Ask yourself whether you are allocating sufficient time to Him in order to allow you to spend eternity with Him down the road.

DEEPEN YOUR TRUST IN GOD

- Chart out and analyze two weeks of your time.
- Question your habits.
- Challenge yourself to devote more time to God.
- Get/Stay active with your preferred place of worship.
- Read the Bible every day.
- Let your life's actions reflect your intentions.

CHAPTER 6

DON'T BE AFRAID

Throughout the Bible the comforting phrase "Do not be afraid" can be found in over 100 places. The phrase is spoken repeatedly by many Biblical figures. Why do you think the phrase is so prevalent? It's because God knows that we experience anxiety when we agonize over our toughest struggles. Job loss, broken relationships, financial disarray, uncertainty, death of a loved one or serious health conditions can worsen our fears. God is aware of our insecurities, so He tries to reassure us that He is always there to provide guidance, comfort and inspiration.

Start with the resources God has made available to you. The Bible is not an intimidating, radical book. It is a practical book with insights that can help you resolve your concerns. There are countless stories and teachings that mirror any dilemmas you face. Do a little research and make sure you pick a translation that is easy to understand so that you can grasp the context and significance of what you are reading. God is ready to speak to you if you let Him.

Your weapons against fear often include the people nearest to you. People who know you well can be your best counselors. If you have anxiety or fear that is nagging beneath the surface of your life, they are more likely to notice it. Be open to their comments and gentle guidance. Be aware that God may send you selected sources of encouragement, such as placing people in your life at crucial times. Look for God's underlying message through conversation, interaction and prayer.

A lawyer friend of mine was feeling the financial pressures of meeting the payroll in his big office. One day, his mind racing from distress and lost in his own concerns, he got on the elevator in his office building. At first, he barely noticed a woman next to him mumbling to herself. He expected to reach his floor without engaging with her. Instead, the woman started pouring out her heart . . . and he listened. She was a widow and she had no money to pay her expenses, including her husband's funeral. She blurted out in exasperation, "Why is God letting this happen to me?" Befuddled, my friend had no good answer. Then the woman answered her own question for both of them. "God is going to walk me through this and He's going to be with me every step of the way," she said. "So I'll rely on Him for my answers." The silk-stocking lawyer learned a lesson that day about how to be fearless when you place your faith in God.

God offers us something else to combat fear. We can directly petition Him for help. Try it. Say a prayer and request God's help with a problem. Visualize God standing next to you, perhaps with His hand on your shoulder. Ask Him out loud to lift the fear from your mind. Say the phrase "Do not be afraid" as if God were speaking it to you. Imagine God whispering in your ear that He is with you, and abandon your fear. Ask Him to lead and direct you in your upcoming decisions. Trust Him and He will afford you the courage to willingly accept whatever outcomes await you. God may be willing to allow you to experience hardships, but He also plans to be by your side every step of the way. Make room for Him and your doubt will be consumed by your courage.

Years ago, my mom recommended a book titled *Medjugorje: The*

Message, by Wayne Weible. Weible was a journalist who went to a tiny village in the mountains of Yugoslavia to report on six children who claimed to have received nightly visits from the Blessed Virgin Mary since June 1981.

Weible's experiences and observations, particularly coming from a journalist who was skeptical of Marian apparition claims, were deeply moving. While reading the book, I found guidance to improve my own prayer life. My life had lost some of its direction and I sought renewal. One evening, I let loose with a request to God to open me up to whatever direction He planned for my life.

Then, that evening I had a vivid dream. I found myself in a setting of indescribable tranquility. Peace radiated from what felt like every pore of my body. In the distance, I saw a figure drawing closer. As she approached, I could see it was the Blessed Virgin Mary, bathed in an aura of holiness. When she got to me, she said, "Do not be afraid." But I wasn't afraid. I was in a state of unimaginable ease. As majestically as she arrived, she departed past the horizon. I awoke with an indescribable sense of peace. I began to focus on eliminating fear and anxiety and grew more confident in trusting God for outcomes. I prayed more often and with deeper obedience to follow God's message. I encourage you to do the same. Your life will change and you'll experience less fear and anxiety. Trust God to lead and guide you. He will, if you open yourself to His creativity.

Some people are unable to conquer their fear of death. They spend endless and needless hours worrying about the unknown and unknowable. That is understandable because death is scary. It is unavoidable. Eventually, each of us will die. But this knowledge does not need to terrify you. The pages of Scripture are full of examples of God's absolute power over death. Read and believe the Bible and you will find relief from your fear.

When you trust God, you have nothing to fear. Simply pass your worries over to Him. Leave the concerns about tomorrow safely behind by spending more time in prayer. Know you are in God's hands. Stop being consumed with the timing and nature of your own demise. Don't give the devil the ability to entangle your thoughts in paralyzing fright. If you allow your concern about death to consume you, you have less to offer in life. God can see your troubled heart and He knows that you can push through your gloom to see the glory that lies ahead. As your trust in God grows, you will find that death need not be such an overwhelming concern.

Most of our experiences with death do not revolve around our own passing. When someone we love dies, it creates a void in our lives. We are forced to react when death impacts someone close to us. Lives are disrupted. Relationships with family and friends get turned upside down. It can feel difficult to interact with those directly impacted by loss. It is hard to endure that level of emotional distress. Avoidance is not the answer. People who grieve can be comforted by hearing stories of their loved ones or by quiet condolence. Your grace will engulf those who are trying to adapt to a loss. As you might expect, the greatest helper is often the person who can sit in silence with another as they grieve.

When you communicate with people in mourning, say a prayer beforehand and ask God to provide the right words. Reflect on the life of the deceased. Ask God to bless and forgive their soul. Consider what the person who passed would hope to convey to those left behind. Then let God do the rest: the words will come. You can share the thought of your loved one, hand in hand with God, entering the heavenly kingdom of peace. One day you will join them and joyfully celebrate a heartfelt reunion.

It is almost unthinkable when people die at an early age. Experiencing such a death is traumatic and the search for understanding is more difficult. We knew of a mother who had to bury a child. The traumatic events surrounding the death had caused the mother to lose faith in God. However, she chose to have a Christian burial. At the service, the minister spoke directly to her and said that her choice of a faith-based funeral was her first step back to a trusting relationship with Christ. If she trusted God, she would see her son again. What beauty in a time of great loss!

It is not easy to trust God when such deaths occur. The devil exists and his goal is to constantly confuse, tempt and promote poor decisions, which have a profound effect on us and innocent bystanders. Sometimes a good reason for a person's death cannot be discerned and we have to ask God to help us through such times. Perhaps God sees certain people as too pure for this life, or their unique mission on this earth has already been achieved with meaningful outcomes to follow. Even in sadness, your life must move forward and you will need to make a conscious effort to embrace life as God intended.

Learn to see the passing of life as a reward to enter into God's kingdom, not as a punishment to you or the deceased. Envision the peacefulness we will experience when we join God and see our loved ones again, smiling joyously. Remove worrisome thoughts of death with a vision of God warmly smiling at you and embracing your deceased loved one. Allow God to be in control of your life. Let Him decide when your time or another's time on earth will cease. We often take people for granted and don't appreciate them until after a death. Strengthen your relationships with others each day and maximize your enjoyment of them here and now. Leave death to God and do not be afraid to live each day to its fullest.

DEEPEN YOUR TRUST IN GOD

- When you trust God, you have nothing to fear.
- Request God's help with specific problems.
- God has power over death.
- Do not be consumed with thoughts of death.
- Make sure to find time to spend with those suffering a great loss.
- The words will come.

CHAPTER 7

FORGIVE AND LET GO

Forgiving someone is one of the most difficult actions we ask of ourselves. Movies and our broader culture largely promote revenge as the proper response when we are wronged. We want to strike back. We want those who have wronged us to suffer as we did. Being wounded is so demoralizing that our initial impulse is often to seek vengeance. Our righteous anger festers. But the longer you let such thoughts remain, the harder it will be to forgive.

Learning to be more forgiving will change your approach to life. Start with your loved ones. Those closest to us are often the instigators of our personal disappointments. If you focus on diminishing your dissatisfactions with others, their displeasing actions will become less prominent in your mind. When offended, try saying a simple prayer asking God to remove your grudge and not only restore but strengthen the relationship. Usually our loved ones are not trying to hurt us, so we should offer them the benefit of the doubt. People make mistakes. When we resist the urge to expect one hundred percent perfection from others, we protect our relationships from deteriorating.

A close friend of mine was the victim of a demanding father who constantly placed unrealistic expectations on the whole family. The father was a financially successful, hard-driving perfectionist who never acknowledged when he did something wrong. He was unsparing when others let him down, particularly his son. When the father passed away, my friend learned some hard truths, including previously undiscovered financial and emotional messes. His father had done some awful things and now, a year later, there was no way to confront the deceased about his behavior. My friend was distraught and had no room in his heart to forgive his father, which seemed to make perfect sense to him. I prayed to God for the right words. I was inspired to share with my friend that his issues were not about his father, but about himself. Even though the data justified his bitter view of his old man, that resentment was eroding his inner soul, so forgiveness would be an act of self-preservation. A few months later, it was so rewarding to witness the return of my good friend's joyous demeanor when he started on the path to mercy.

Forgiving others freely is an act of spiritual maturity and provides an example to others. It is about healing your own heart. It does not mean that you give up your belief system. When someone seeks forgiveness from you, willingly provide it and allow that person to be healed. If you are expecting an apology and one is not forthcoming, try not to redirect anger at those closest to you. Procrastination will not heal the rift. Harboring negative thoughts about those who hurt you is detrimental to your sound mental health. Seek out the original transgressor and initiate a conversation. Let the offender know that something serious is bothering you and you need their help resolving it. Use a conciliatory tone as you explain how their actions or words have hurt you. Let the person who wronged you express themselves. If an apology is offered, accept it with humility and proceed quickly to reconciliation. You won't regret it.

When you are the one who has committed the wrong, get in front of it. Seek a meeting as soon as possible with the one you injured. Be sincere in your words and deliberate in your apology. This is not a time for backpedaling. Simply share how your heart aches from the breach in your relationship and how you hope this apology opens the door to healing. Do not justify your actions or re-litigate the incident.

Your tone must be sincere, honest and humble. If you feel you might stumble or botch the apology in person, write a letter. Some of the raw emotions of a meeting are absent when you send a letter. Having a chance to put it all down on paper can clarify your thoughts and help you focus on what you must say. The letter can lead to an eventual meeting without emotional outbursts.

All my life I have enjoyed practical jokes. By the time I was in college there were not many boundaries I would not cross to "get" somebody good. The resident advisor in our dorm was a priest, one of the good ones, whom I admired. There are certain impactful people in my life. When I disappoint them, I feel guilty. This priest was one of those impactful people. One night, I was leaning a bucket of water on his door when he suddenly opened the door. I tried to relieve the situation by insisting that I was only joking, but I could tell he was hurt. I felt terrible about it. What if God had opened that door with that disappointing look on His face? It ate at me. Even as I became a more mature Christian, I cringed at the memory.

Years later, I had the opportunity to see the priest again. I apologized for my immature behavior and begged his forgiveness. He insisted that the past actions of a juvenile were long forgotten and no bad feelings had survived. He insisted that I turn over my embarrassment to God and let it go. He forgave me without pause or qualification. And then, it was over. Years of personal guilt melted away. What an example of forgiveness it was for me. I thanked God for the priest's willingness to openly forgive, and I determined to mirror those same actions when I was called upon to forgive another. In general, it's much easier for the recipient to accept an apology that is genuinely offered in a timely manner.

Sometimes when an insult takes place, each party blames the other. Both sides stubbornly refuse to offer an apology. When this occurs, pray over the dilemma and ask God to guide you. It takes even greater courage to request forgiveness when you believe you are not at fault. Initiate the apology. Look the person in the eye, choose simple words of regret and offer your apology in heartfelt and calm tones. You won't regret it. Don't allow your pride and stubbornness to delay forgiveness. That only results in harming your inner self and hurting others. Take the action and be amazed at how quickly the damaged bridges are repaired.

When you exhibit stubbornness by withholding forgiveness from others, innocent bystanders may feel the impact, particularly loved ones who must endure your harbored disdain. As you reflect on the power of genuine forgiveness, ask God to inspire your words of apology. Eliminate hesitation and be sincere. When it comes to forgiveness, keep your approach simple. God willingly forgives us. Shouldn't we do the same for others?

DEEPEN YOUR TRUST IN GOD

- The longer you wait, the harder it is to forgive.
- Forgiveness lightens the burden on both sets of shoulders.
- Accept the apologies of others with humility.
- Offer your own apology with sincerity.
- Offer forgiveness, even when you think the offense was not your fault.
- Be timely when you offer contrition.

CHAPTER 8

LET GOD JUDGE

I t is easy to judge others. We live a certain way, so we think others should mirror us. We want people to act and think as we do. When others don't handle a situation as we would, we often demean their response. If we think we know the circumstances, we often pass severe judgement on someone's actions, not bothering to consider that they may have acted out of character or were overwhelmed by circumstances. We rarely consider that the person may have simply seen the circumstances differently, because by then, we are often busy ridiculing that person to another friend. If God judged you the way you judge others, what would happen?

When you judge others, it implies you have the authority to do so. But who gave you that authority? Your ego. Are you sure you want that authority? If you witness or experience an injustice, don't worry that God is missing something or requires your assistance. Trust that He will respond in His way on His timetable. Withholding judgment does not mean you ignore wrongful or hurtful actions. Our judicial system assigns punishment every day to guilty people in civil and criminal court. If you witness a wrongful act, be a good citizen and report the wrongdoing, offering support to the proper authorities who will deliver justice.

Remove the judging of others from your personal habits. There is nothing wrong with having a passionate disagreement with another, but we need to be fully aware of the damage we cause others and ourselves when we judge. Our harsh takedown demoralizes the recipient and eats at their self-worth. Don't allow your own ego to be judge and jury of another. Denigrating someone's weaknesses to validate your position is not a practice worthy of God. It may be your own insecurity on display with your harsh rebuke of others during difficult encounters. If someone is treating you with cruelty, don't you think God knows that? Trust God to handle your dilemma His way. Further, seek His guidance in how you think He wants you to respond.

One time when my family and I moved to a new neighborhood, I was greeted by a next-door neighbor who was a rough, gruff, sarcastic older man. He took some gratuitous verbal shots at my favorite college team. Our exchange was so caustic that later, when I sat with my wife, I explained that we were certain to have troubles with this crank for years to come. I was wrong. The man ended up being a helpful and fun neighbor who protected and watched over our kids as though they were his own. He gave great advice and took on the role of informal grandfather in our family. Fifteen years later, when he and his wife put up a "For Sale" sign to move to a retirement community, our children, not wanting them to leave, took the sign down!

As you refrain from judging others, your life will begin to let go of your habitual hurtful words or strong reactions. Disdain for others will dissipate and your heart will open up to inner peace and deeper insights into the value of those in your life. Your family and friends will be motivated by your new take on things. Not judging others is infectious and your new habit will encourage others to do likewise. Leave the judging to God and you'll find your heart replacing bitterness and envy with joy, serenity and understanding.

DEEPEN YOUR TRUST IN GOD

- Leave judging others to God.
- Personal pride prevents proper perspective.
- Harsh words and strong reactions crush others.
- Quit your job as captain of the behavior police.
- Refrain from judging others.
- Motivate your friends and family with your new approach.

CHAPTER 9

JESUS ...
LOOK AGAIN

J esus is the single most influential figure in world history. If you
doubt that, check your calendar. Jesus is the most awe-inspiring
individual that mankind will ever know. The story of His life and
the teachings from His lips have rewritten human history. If Jesus is
so influential in our world, shouldn't we want to know more about
Him? The teachings of Christ may cause us some level of discomfort,
but they are fundamentally simple guidelines for loving God and
serving others.

Jesus was born into a world of great turmoil. The state had
overwhelming authority. Violence was common. People worshipped
many pagan gods. Only the Jewish faith was monotheistic, but it
represented only five percent of the population. Jesus was raised in
the Jewish tradition and became a rabbi and teacher. The followers of
Jesus included many martyrs, and through them His message spread.
The result is that now the majority of people believe there is one
true God. Such an incredibly influential feat forces us to ask what it
means for today.

Jesus focused on two major concepts. The first was honoring God and living your life in a manner that is pleasing to Him. The second was treating others as you wish to be treated. Sounds simple but that was the focus of all His amazing works. Jesus taught us how to worship God and how to treat one another. These two principles pervade the Ten Commandments and Old Testament Jewish law, and led to a new covenant that was created through the death and resurrection of Jesus. So here we are, some 2,000 years later, and we have the benefit of observing how Jesus changed the world. As you reflect on Jesus' presence on earth, persuade yourself to learn more about Him. I have many Christian and Jewish friends and, although I am not schooled sufficiently to distinguish all the differences in our core beliefs, I challenge myself and others to learn more about the teachings of Jesus to help build bridges that increase mutual understanding.

I will never forget the vision I had one evening that inspired my faith. I dreamed I was kneeling in a chapel, praying with twenty or so people. There was an altar and a priest at a table. Out of nowhere, a young boy around the age of twelve appeared by the priest's side. The boy then slowly turned to the congregation and a brilliant light shot forth from his chest, emanating out to all and piercing the hearts of those in attendance. My entire body filled with indescribable peace and my heart was beating vibrantly, but not painfully. I was overcome with joy. I bolted straight up in bed, wide awake and curious about what I had dreamed. Was this an inspiration to live a more childlike life of trust and faith in God? Was that little boy just a child encouraging me to learn more? Perhaps it was the Teacher himself! Look again at the signals and signs guiding you, and transform how you are living your life.

I prayed and asked God for insight. I was curious about the young boy, so I asked God. Immediately, the name of Jesus entered my mind and I thanked God for providing that thought. I sought guidance about my proper response. God filled me with inspiring thoughts and encouragements that remain with me today. My experience was certainly memorable and I was deeply affected by witnessing the Holy Spirit that closely. Perhaps these writings are the net result.

We have to help others open their minds to how God interacts with us daily, and we must open ourselves to deeper prayer and learning. I am convinced that if each of us became more committed to honoring God in our homes, workplaces, neighborhoods and cities, the world would become a more joyful and rewarding place to live.

Brandon, a popular guy, grew up in an environment with minimal religious involvement. At age seventeen, he transferred to a Christian high school to play basketball with an eye towards earning a college scholarship. After a year at the school, Brandon was not fitting in with these kids who were living their lives based on Christian principles. He could not get used to how amicably they interacted with fellow students and even strangers. Caring people seemed pretty weird to him. But the only way to get that basketball scholarship was to stick around another season. Brandon decided to stay and "look again." He achieved his dream. He went on to play college basketball but he also took a second look at the teachings of love, hope and concern for your neighbor that his teammates and teachers embodied. He now plans a career working with young people in ministry!

Jesus spent much of his time with those who struggled with life. His lessons were rarely complex: Assist others in need. Ask forgiveness from those you wrong. Encourage others. Respect and care for loved ones. Be a good friend. Don't mock others. Don't gossip. Defend the unjustly accused. Share. Be humble. Be thankful. Jesus's message was empowered with hope, the driving force that stimulates you to face each day and prepare for tomorrow. A faith-filled approach to life will lead you to trust God more, and guide your life to happiness and satisfaction. Jesus demonstrated limitless benevolence, forgiveness, humility and sincerity. When you follow Him, love will overwhelm your heart and wisdom will fill your mind. Seek Him and practice the joy of His teachings in your everyday life.

Use daily prayer as your most effective tool to stay connected to Jesus. Each day is an opportunity to improve upon yesterday and become a better person. Allow the care of Jesus and the love of God to inspire you each morning, and you will find it easier to devote your time to assisting others physically, emotionally, intellectually and spiritually. Let Him be your primary source of influence and you will be better prepared to share God with others when the need arises. Jesus has done the difficult work; you merely need to share the good news.

DEEPEN YOUR TRUST IN GOD

- Change your outlook.
- Jesus commands us to honor God first.
- Treat others as though they were accompanied by God.
- Share the good news of Jesus with others.
- As your knowledge of Jesus deepens, your life improves.
- Live Jesus' message.

CHAPTER 10

TEMPTATION, YOUR NEMESIS

Have you ever taken a moment to reflect on what influences your thoughts, including people and devices? Our minds grow from what we experience. Your surroundings impact how you think and act. Remember those early computer geeks and their old adage, "Garbage in, garbage out."? Your thoughts reflect what you see, hear and experience.

Excessive exposure to violence, profanity, pornography, internet sites, chat rooms and so much other content can be damaging. Friends and family can also, at times, be the wrong kind of influence. Our lives are full of temptation. The traps—poor decisions, selfishness, envy, vulgarity and all manner of addictions—await our slightest misstep every day. Clearly, these thoughts and actions are inspired by the evil one.

The devil exists and tempts us continuously. He is the generator of all evil. He knows your weaknesses and he exploits them. The devil's primary objective is to entice you to make poor and selfish decisions that weaken your reliance on God. Some of his work is obvious, but other times he operates in subtle and deceptive ways, slowly eroding your values over time. He is patient in his work because he knows our vanity will create opportunities for him.

It is now so easy to be inundated by inappropriate behavior, frequently through quite mainstream and acceptable forms of entertainment. The result is that we become immune to lewd behavior. The level of respect that people hold for others and themselves has decreased, and selfishness has become a virtue in many minds. Our failure to confront this moral erosion in a sustained way is pushing us further away from God and His plan for us.

Involving yourself in compromising environments will erode your morals and weaken the shield that protects what is pure in your heart. I remember a time when a friend invited me to an all-guys' party. It sounded like the perfect way to blow off steam. I wasn't totally shocked when a stripper showed up, but I had not anticipated it, either. Most of the guys were married. I felt instantly uncomfortable but I was paralyzed by uncertainty about how to react. I briefly separated from the group and said a quick prayer for guidance. I didn't want to make a scene, but I wanted to do the right thing. Suddenly, I felt powerfully encouraged to leave the party, so I quietly stepped outside and headed home. On my way home, I felt better about leaving, although I still debated whether I should have said or done something more. Afterwards, I committed myself to avoiding such encounters in the future. Now I always ask a question or two about certain invitations, and when similar temptations arise unexpectedly, I just say "No, thanks." And sometimes that is not the most popular response, but I have also seen other guys reject similar offers after they see me take that stand.

Our entertainment industry continues to push the envelope of vulgarity, violence and sexual extremes. Games, shows, chat lines, computer programs and videos compete almost without limits to shock us and titillate viewers with a river of toxic sludge. Our latest technological breakthroughs offer devices with even easier access to deplorable content, so you shouldn't be surprised when you or your acquaintances behave in ways that are eerily similar to something you have read or witnessed. Our thoughts and actions are reflections of what we see, hear and discuss. Our habits tend to conform to what we consistently view.

Our world is filled with constant temptation. I recall a guy who was struggling with watching pornographic videos. He finally convinced himself to share his embarrassment with a good friend. To his surprise, his friend was having the same dilemma and didn't know who to talk to about it. They both sought to defeat this nasty habit that they had failed to overcome on their own. By sharing their weakness with one another, both were motivated and compelled to help each other, rather than focus on themselves. Their genuine concern for each other allowed them to make it a team effort. They spoke openly about how uncomfortable they felt knowing they would one day be required to explain such actions to God. They were forced to rely on one another to manage a problem that neither could conquer alone. Sometimes, success will be easier for you if you are trying to get your buddy over the finish line. Friends and loved ones are conduits to God. Have the courage to ask a friend for support in overcoming a persistent and corrosive temptation. Pray for them and yourself, asking God to inspire you to greater accountability.

You have to be constantly on guard, not only for yourself but also for your loved ones. Sometimes the battle can feel overwhelming. Our daily media options heavily promote degrading behavior to the point that we are exposed to immoral material, often without seeking it out. We become immune to lewd behavior and we begin to accept such actions as normal. How disappointed God must be with our acceptance of today's evil and selfishness. We need to conscientiously focus on objecting to these growing influences that are engulfing our society. That work begins with you.

When our children were younger and first wanted to view inappropriate movies, we had arguments over it. They were experiencing peer pressure to watch those movies, and they were embarrassed to have parents who would not permit them to go. We seemed so unreasonable to them because the very popular movies were often on our list of unacceptable movies. My wife read some advice about how to address the situation and we tried it. I posed a simple question to the kids: if someone makes you a fresh plate of brownies but they prepare the tasty treats with just "a little bit of dog poop," would you eat it? "Dad, that's gross," was the firm reply. We shared how viewing certain content was no different. If you expose your mind to virtual dog poop, your mind will digest it and it becomes a part of you. So be strong, deny the evil one's temptations, and keep the dog poop out of your brownies!

Public trust and acknowledgement of God is diminishing. Opposition to God in our government structure is rampant. Our great country was founded by men who publicly sought God's favor in the establishment of our government. Our forefathers framed their debates with each other in spiritual and moral terms. They understood that an amoral populace would not survive long under the unique obligations that liberty demands. Leaders now offer a mere tip of the hat to God when closing their secular speeches, but they often show little evidence that their decisions are based on firm morality. Our forefathers were outwardly faithful and recognized the role of God in governance. We need to become better at that.

The devil will never cease to promote selfishness and meanness in our society. Evil is extremely intelligent and manipulative, and if you are going to combat it, you must spot it early and challenge it loudly.

The devil knows and will exploit your weaknesses, so be ready to confront and reject his temptations each day. When your conscience remains silent in the presence of inappropriate behavior, you devalue your own belief system. If you fail to recognize the devil's false but enticing fruits, you stand a good chance of allowing his works to germinate within your mind. Appreciate that the devil is patient and willing to take as much time as he needs to subtly weaken your standards and society's fabric. He knows that a gradual degradation of standards will eventually give birth to a new normal, creating a society indifferent to despicable behavior and too splintered to know how to fight back.

Your temptations are a wound that, if neglected, becomes infected. If you continue to neglect the wound it can worsen, leading to surgery or loss of a limb or organ, or even death. You wouldn't ignore a critical medical condition, so treat your temptations no differently. Seek immediate help to cure them and don't allow your personal weakness to complicate the proper treatment of your symptoms. Disavow your stubbornness, pride or ignorance, all of which can spin out of control leading to spiritual demise. Trust God to heal all of your habitual wounds of temptation and poor actions. God is the healer of all wounds.

In combating evil, the first step is to recognize that God did not create it. Many Christians wonder why God allows it. Perhaps God allows evil to see how well we respond to it. Please do not get lost in this debate with others. If you believe God provides all the good in your life and loves you, then it stands to reason that He isn't the one initiating the negative temptations and discouraging interactions in your life. There is no doubt that the devil exists and that he is hard at work, tempting us all hours of every day.

The devil's earliest dodge is to blame God for the stubborn presence of evil in this world. If he can plant in your head a feeling that somehow God is not properly managing events, he has won a significant victory: he has clouded your judgment about the nature of evil. Over time, as your moral compass becomes less reliable, the devil will unrelentingly feed you more reasons to doubt. As you succumb to these temptations, you could steer your life in a direction where more degrading choices await you. That is the fight we are all in.

Even in areas of our lives where we may be operating with best intentions, our vulnerability to temptation exists. Of course, there is nothing inherently wrong with trying to achieve greater financial gain, increased influence and authority, better schools for your kids or public recognition for your work. You may be an expert at winning an argument or seeking more physical pleasure in your life. However, are you going about achieving these goals in a way that is appropriate? The devil hopes to push your interest in these things to the point of an obsession or distraction from your spiritual life. When you fall short of your goals, he will manipulate your frustration and anger. When you succeed in these goals, he will appeal to your vanity and arrogance. We have been empowered to discern right from wrong, but sometimes the less obvious wrongs take much longer to recognize.

Another subtle trick of the devil is to slowly separate us from our place of worship. Have you ever become less engaged in a religious service because you got to know your pastor or rabbi better and, with that deeper familiarity, got to know his flaws? Maybe there is some piece of doctrine that has come down from the national leadership that rubs you the wrong way.

Or perhaps there's a person who sits near you and their behavior or demeanor irritates you. Perhaps you view the music program as weak, or you find the children's service annoying. Are you too critical of the message that was delivered and how it was presented and interpreted? This can go on and on and on until one day, you wake up and tell yourself there may be far better ways to spend your time than attending your house of worship, which now you might consider to be a house of hypocrites.

Temptation is a formidable weapon and the devil is prepared to use it in obvious ways (porn, promiscuity, greed, vanity, false gods) and subtle ways (ambition, lethargy, despair) which can all be snares in your attempt to live righteously. Don't panic. See the desires and thoughts racing in your head for what they are: unwelcome guests. Knowing that the evil one exists and that his goal is to erode your beliefs is half the battle.

Have you ever stopped and reflected on why you accept selfish and immoral behavior as normal, and refuse to discern right from wrong? Our consciences are constantly faced with making decisions that require quick responses without considering the negative ramifications that can arise. Confrontations can be as simple as responding to someone cutting you off in traffic, being the recipient of a mean comment or gesture, or facing your weakness or addiction. When you are placed in such situations, recognize the devil and his temptations. If you want to participate in God's way, challenge yourself to stand up for what you believe in your heart is morally sound, and refuse to surrender to the negative thoughts that confront you each day.

One helpful visual I was taught to use when I faced uncomfortable situations, such as criticizing someone else's behavior or viewing something I shouldn't, is to imagine what my conversation looks like to God. Inevitably, when I consider God's perspective, I quickly grow uncomfortable and look for ways to stop myself from judging others, so I try to change the subject or refrain from adding more fuel. Over time, I make more conscious efforts to avoid people who lead me into the trap of gossip with their cunning questions and whispered putdowns. If you don't contemplate the damage to others because of your actions, who will?

Another goal is to remove the sources that generate temptations in your life and instead enable your thoughts and actions to align with God's will. What you expose your mind to directly influences your decision-making. We choose what we absorb. Be wary and recognize that your habits will conform to what you consistently view. You must do a content inventory of your life. Remove the sources of temptation. Television shows, internet sites, chat lines, Twitter, jokes and inappropriate books can all do damage. Take a minute and list the obvious sources right now on a piece of paper. Request God's intervention directly with these stubborn foes and then burn the list, thus releasing yourself from its power. Say a prayer and ask God to help you defeat and remove your unwanted temptations. Bad habits can be broken with prayer, family support, new activities and personal determination. When you name them specifically, they become more visible to you as you seek to clean them out.

Periodically, I find myself tempted to engage in activities that expose my weaknesses. When I fail to resist, I then try to formulate a better plan to avoid the same old temptation next time. Pay attention to the circumstances that lead you into the inevitable mistakes.

As you identify and remove negative behaviors from your life, fill the void with productive and richer activities, which is God's intention for your life. As you make more morally sound decisions, you will find yourself less comfortable in the previous patterns and you will seek correction earlier and earlier, until the temptation remains outside of you with no invitation to come closer. God protects the sincere heart. Seek His involvement. He's there. You just have to grasp it!

I started a new routine while dressing for work. I listen to eight to ten minutes of inspirational materials while getting ready. I choose from a wide variety of refreshing and educational viewpoints. It improves my focus before starting the rush of the day. At night, I like to read a page or two from an inspirational reading, whether it be a book, the Bible, a spiritual program or article. I find that filling my mind at the beginning and end of each day with an inspiring insight sharpens my focus on God's plan for me.

Use the internet to find spiritual and influential articles. I'm signed up with a website that emails me a daily scripture, plus its interpretation and a prayer. It takes me a minute or two to read. Regularly fortifying your mind with positive and motivational material sharpens your discernment and makes spotting temptations easier. Be a tough gatekeeper of the material that enters your mind, and have the conviction to turn off a program that is degrading or immoral. I don't have to watch every movie or TV show to know if they are bad for me. It is easier to lock out negative thoughts using some simple screening: look for those daily resources that will replace your previous, questionable content. In this effort, the multibillion-dollar entertainment industry is not always your friend.

Another habit I have employed is to forward inspiring messages to my friends. I find joy and support in these articles and enjoy sharing my experience. Encouraging each other is so rewarding and easy to do. When you share your positive discoveries with others, they are uplifted and you are spiritually reinforced. Your friends in God remain some of the most vital resources for your transformation.

I sometimes wonder if God shakes His head in wonder over our hyper-organized and hyper-stimulated lives. We seek very little "evidence" of God's presence in our lives and we find precious few minutes to ever contemplate it. Yet, the whole wide world is a spellbinding masterpiece of creation, so let's find time to appreciate it more. Haven't there been moments in your life when you were caught up in the awesome beauty of nature? Have you sat alone listening to the wind through the trees or a rainstorm or a rustling creek? Could you describe the majesty of a fresh blanket of snow or the roar of the ocean to someone who had seen or heard neither? When the sun hits your face on a cool autumn day, what goes through your mind? Nature's beauty is breathtaking and it will humble you. It's a constant source of uplifting inspirations that only requires your time to view and appreciate. Nevertheless, unhappy people are stomping around complaining of the lack of "evidence" of God.

Most of us take for granted the source of our daily food and drink. If we spent more time acknowledging that most of the things we consume are derived from God's gift of the field or through rainfall, we might have a better appreciation for how God provides for us physically, mentally and spiritually every day. When reflecting on life, contemplate how nature interacts with your journey, just like branches connected to a tree. There are many existing species of trees in endless sizes and leaf colors. Yet each tree, even those of the same species, is uniquely shaped. Their branches reach out in many directions.

Tree growth is influenced by the quality of the tree's foundation, other surrounding plant life and resources provided by God. Some trees find themselves in poor growing conditions because of rocky soil, limited sunlight or insufficient water. Yet the tree can survive, often with a little help from humans. Likewise, you can clear away the weeds and shadows that cause your personal shortcomings, and push yourself to new heights and sources of inspiration. That mighty oak in the forest will be you.

DEEPEN YOUR TRUST IN GOD

- The devil is attempting to make a claim on your heart.
- Be clear-eyed in spotting temptation.
- Carefully evaluate what you watch, see and hear.
- Ask God to defeat unwanted temptations.
- Find daily inspirational material and share it with others.
- Picture God sitting next to you when you view objectionable content.

CHAPTER 11

GET IN THE GAME

D o you enjoy the camaraderie that accompanies observing or participating in an athletic event, great concert or special party? When we spend quality time with others, it is enjoyable and deepens our bonds with one another. Attending a worship service, be it church, temple or mosque, should be viewed no differently. Active involvement in a worship service deepens your connection to others while it satisfies you spiritually. When you sincerely display your faith publicly, you demonstrate God's importance in your life and invite others to do the same. Publicly honoring God is extremely important to Him. If it weren't, He would not have included it as one of His Ten Commandments.

Weekly worship is designed to keep an uninterrupted flow of God's blessings in your life. Many of my family and friends do not attend a regular service. Some of my kids in college and recent graduates don't attend Mass. I pray and search for ways to encourage them without turning them further away. I worry about it and ask God to open their hearts to the inspirational rewards of consistent attendance. I recently shared my concern with a friend, and he insisted without hesitation that I should not fret. He explained that my kids and friends are still on the team, just not in the game right now. Continuing his sports analogy, he said they are on the sidelines and to get on the field they must aspire to practice. They have to want it. The more you practice your faith and educate yourself, the better you become. He encouraged me to pray for them to do just that and trust God to intercede. Everyone likes to get in the game sooner or later, he noted, especially because God's game provides the ultimate reward: the key to eternity!

When attending a worship service, don't just check the box indicating you showed up. Get in the game. Mere attendance results in meager rewards. Beyond the great fellowship, attending a worship service permits you to deepen your understanding of and relationship with God. Preparation is often the key. Have you ever taken a few moments to properly prepare your heart and mind for a message?

Almost always, from a bulletin or online, you can get the upcoming readings and sermon title prior to the service. Devote some time prior to the service for reading the scriptures that your pastor plans to share. Devote a few minutes prior to the service meditating on the subject at hand. When I do this, I tend to be more attuned to the message and the whole experience affects me on a deeper level.

As you enter the worship service, clear your mind with an immediate prayer that God will open you to this message and this moment. This is only one to three hours of your time in a week, so don't squander it with a bad attitude or worries about other things. Stay focused. You are there to learn and be coached, so bring your best game. For each service, set a goal of learning something new and reinforcing something meaningful, particularly if you've heard it before.

Seeds cannot grow in a poorly tended field. If your focus dims during a sermon, try to reclaim it with a quick prayer. It could be as simple as "God, please help me to listen, concentrate and grasp the words being spoken today." A much-admired priest, Father Ted, used to encourage us all to simply pray "Come, Holy Spirit."

Try not to blame yourself when you fail to grasp the point of the various messengers you will hear over time. Not all pastors will be great orators. Ask God to improve your attention span if you are listening to a dull recitation. Make it a game of finding the truth under all of that fertilizer.

A key moment for anybody trying to get the most out of a worship service occurs when you leave. After you have said your goodbyes to all around, find a quiet moment to reflect on what was said. Summarize the themes in one or two sentences, and reflect on how you can incorporate those lessons into your life. If you leave a service with no clear message in mind, perhaps it means that you allowed the distractions of the day to overwhelm your focus.

As you drive home, discuss the message with family members. Hearing their perspectives expands my understanding, but also helps me absorb parts of the message that I may have missed. Review the utility of the day's devotional to everyone's current situation. I always want to figure out how to apply the message to my life. When our children were younger, we made a game of this practice by asking questions, like we were playing a trivia game. We always praised good answers and occasionally treated the kids to something special when they embraced the messages or identified practical applications. Keep it light and focus on the message, but always work to encourage your children to become improved players of God's game.

Irvin was a good friend and co-worker who enjoyed a hearty laugh that would cause anyone within earshot to laugh or smile. One day he shared with me that he had been diagnosed with cancer. He was a big teddy bear of a man, but now he was afraid. He believed in God but did not necessarily possess a strong faith or regularly attend a service. While I was in church praying for Irvin, I came across a book called *My Daily Bread*. I saw this as a sign, bought the book and gave it to Irvin, encouraging him to read it, perhaps a few pages a day. Irvin soon embraced the book and his trust and outlook changed. He found incredible joy and his attitude improved noticeably. His insight and willingness to share his thoughts were inspiring. Despite struggling with cancer that ultimately resulted in surgery, Irvin's laugh never faded and only became more contagious. He had come off the bench, studied the playbook and become a fully engaged player on the field.

As the end of his life drew near, Irvin was not the one seeking to be consoled but rather the one providing counsel and words of wisdom for the rest of us. His transformation was heartwarming. When I attended Irvin's wake, the lump in my throat was difficult to swallow as I viewed him peacefully lying with his hands folded, holding *My Daily Bread.* Irvin's quick response to God's playbook inspired me to get better engaged in God's game. I resolved to push myself to become a more educated and better performer on God's turf.

If you are currently not attending a weekly service, ask yourself why. It is clear God wants you there. Your church community is the oxygen that keeps your faith burning bright. Maybe your pastor is boring or not much of a coach. Maybe someone in the service irritates you. If something is holding you back, seek a means for becoming a better player of God's game. You must not let one or a handful of people weaken your beliefs or separate you from God's house.

If something is holding you back, initiate a dialogue with a person in the church that you trust, and reveal your frustrations. If your spiritual leader fails to motivate you, consider approaching him or her personally. They will likely be assisted in communicating better because of your candor. A good pastor is not eager to lose congregants to boredom. These conversations can be difficult, but not backing down from them is a sign of spiritual maturity. Most differences do not warrant a departure.

Can you imagine the expression on God's face if you walk away? Make sure you are not making a change just to get a few extra hours of sleep on Saturay or Sunday, or to support a bad habit. Challenge yourself to provide five reasons for your decision. If you are having difficulty justifying to God why you need to quit your service, embrace that discomfort and let it motivate you to find a better solution. Ironically, one way to improve an unhappy church life is to dig in deeper. Participate in small groups, Bible study, potluck suppers, a homeless outreach and other opportunities that your worship place provides. You may find that you like your spiritual leader a lot more when he is handing you a hammer to build a Habitat for Humanity house.

Perhaps your spiritual understanding has grown more sophisticated and your house of worship no longer feels like a fit. Go about your search for a new worship home in the same way you might look for a job: do some detailed research on the various services that interest you and take the time to visit them. Maybe you have to travel a little farther from home to get to a service that fits you and your family. So what? Try it. Your worship service home should feel like comfortable shoes because it is going to take you on a very long and rewarding journey.

So get in the game. Attending a worship service is a periodic reinforcement of God's guidance in your life, and is one of the vital resources that will help you combat the evil one's temptations. God wants us to follow His lessons and become united with one another through public worship. Consistency of participation is the safest way to ensure God's impact on our lives. When you view worship as merely an obligation, you will leave a service with no more uplift than if you had watched one of your favorite sitcoms. But if you walk through those doors with an open mind, God can flood your heart with love and your mind with wisdom, preparing you for the upcoming week. Then you will experience and benefit from having the home field advantage!

DEEPEN YOUR TRUST IN GOD

- Find a spiritually fulfilling church.
- Attend a weekly worship service.

- Try to regain lost focus with a quick prayer.
- Talk about the sermon on the way home.
- Do not overly concern yourself with the personality of the pastor.
- If you are currently not attending a weekly service, find one.

CHAPTER 12

SMILE ... IT HELPS

Modern life leaves many people overwhelmed, exhausted and filled with anxiety. Too often there are few opportunities to recharge ourselves, which causes frustration, exhaustion and depression. When those around you feel down, you may find it difficult to offer the right guidance to improve their lives. Yet you have in your arsenal a simple, effective weapon: you can offer up a smile. This may seem glib, but hear me out. The smile has great power.

Observe the infectious energy created by a simple smile. It has a magnetic effect that encourages us to build unifying bonds. If you want good friends, you have to *be* a good friend. When you bless treasured people with your best smile, the bonds deepen. A smile conveys an offer of friendliness and help, even if it's just for moral support. A properly placed smile can change a person's outlook from distress to hope. Our society refrains from eye contact and discourages smiling at strangers, and this approach does provide safety from unwanted encounters. However, a simple smile shows that you have a great secret in life: God loves you.

My friend Rick has an incredible impact on almost everyone who enters church. He greets people with gestures ranging from manly handshakes, to high fives for kids, hugs to those needing one and even a slight swat with a song sheet to a young one with an attitude. Every greeting is accompanied by the friendliest smile one can imagine, resulting in returned smiles. I often stand behind him just to brighten my day watching how he changes faces from seriousness, protective cover, sadness, even uncertainty to happiness, relief and a welcoming demeanor. You can feel God smiling back. Rick changes every person's outward appearance—and, I suspect, their inner attitude, too—just by the way he greets and interacts with each one. He transforms how people enter God's house. He is a blessing to us as he demonstrates how friendly smiles can change an outlook and improve a person's day.

When you go around genuinely smiling at people, the effect is disarming. People spend way too much time being defensive. A genuine smile creates positive energy and fortifies bonds of friendship without speaking a word. Smiling is an expression of love and acceptance and a generator of hope and optimism. And when you receive a smile in return, it is a signal of mutual acceptance that brings both people closer together. Smiling protects against discouragement, re-emphasizes the good in life and reminds all that God is at work.

When our daughter was a little girl around preschool age, she had this incredible ability to give someone a smile or hug just when they needed it. My wife and I recall several times that we were walking down the church aisle looking for seats when suddenly our daughter, with these big beautiful blue eyes, would break off and walk into a pew, stretch out her arms and give an older person a big hug and a smile. To observe a stern-looking person suddenly break out in a beaming smile, and in some instances wiping away a tear, created an emotional scene not only for the recipient but also for us and those looking on. What power a smile and a hug pack!

Don't be alarmed if your smile isn't reciprocated. Smiles are inviting but people are not always ready to release their worry at a moment's notice.

Sometimes people just need more time before they become comfortable enough to share their concerns. In the meantime, continue offering them encouragement and pray for them. Let them know that you care about them and are available to help. Your smile suggests friendship, kindness and concern. Smiles are seeds of happiness that sometimes take time to bloom.

When you interact with someone suffering from depression, they often have too much weighing on their mind to engage in conversation. Successful interactions with such people may require more than just a smile. Your string of smiles, over time, can reassure a person that others care, generating the necessary motivation to press forward. I like to support a smile with a quick prayer, asking God to lighten the burden of my troubled friend. I also will ask God for discernment in the situation, so that I may be helpful by guiding someone who needs professional help. Be sensitive and recognize that sometimes a smile is merely the beginning of the help they require.

John shared another story about a complaining waitress who was always grumpy. His friends were customers and often joked with her. One day they broke through her stern armor and she laughed. As the relationship grew, they invited her to a worship service, only to be overwhelmed by her changed spirit. She became an influential messenger of God—all started by a willingness to share smiles.

When you're walking alone, make a practice of looking up to the skies and smiling. Simply say "Thank you" to God for your life and all He is doing within it. Thank Him for the air you breathe and ask for His abundance and mercy in the lives of others. These private moments with God will change your demeanor and attack those worries that haunt you in your quiet moments.

As you know, in this book I have tried to offer you examples from my personal life about each of the lessons I've shared. However, for the section on smiling, I don't need to offer you an example. Each one of us has an example from our own life about an unexpected smile or uplifting encouragement that had a significant and immediate impact. Your infectious smile will help others find their own smile, which in turn will brighten God's smile upon all of us. Witness the joy and satisfaction that accompany a frequent habit of smiling more, and notice how God overwhelms your heart with uplifting happiness.

DEEPEN YOUR TRUST IN GOD

- Your smile is a tool of God.
- Offer your smile with no expectation of reciprocity.
- Smile more.
- Smiling is an expression of love.
- If you see signs of depression, go deeper than a smile.
- When alone, think to smile broadly in God's direction.

CHAPTER 13

REST IN JOY

Adults today find themselves operating with little time for relaxation. Job requirements are more and more demanding. Technological advancements and workplace deficiencies require a quickened pace and a personal workload that produces increasing time pressures. Our social schedules and family activities have us on the go every day. Weekends no longer provide adequate time to relax. Free time gets filled up with family activities or additional work. Our vast entertainment culture provides a large menu of choices and convenient start times. Our social habits drive us to spend our spare time inundated by things to do. In the end, we find ourselves exhausted, leaving little time for God.

Periodically, it's healthy to analyze how and where you spend your leisure time. If you are feeling overly tired, assess your routines and note how much time you allocate towards reading and rest. Chances are, your time management requires some fresh balancing.

My wife and I recently found a new way to refresh ourselves and appreciate God's beauty. We have always enjoyed the spectacular and peaceful majesty captured in a sunset. Just relaxing and watching the sun fall below the horizon, particularly near water, is breathtaking.

We get so overwhelmed by the beauty that God shares in each unique sunset that we feel uplifted and recharged. So we recently made a commitment to view as many sunsets as practical, and the sunsets rarely disappoint. It helps us appreciate God's works of art and inspires us to enjoy life more.

Devote more time to rest and less toward activities. If you have children, the pressures of life often increase exponentially. Many children's activities require parental participation. You should enjoy sharing those experiences with your children, but recognize that if your child's schedule is wearing you out, it may be too much. Be mindful that excessive activities for your kids often replaces genuine opportunities you need to grow closer to them.

Insufficient rest will cause you to become irritable, impatient and lethargic. Those conditions will cause you to run yourself and your family into the ground. If God emphasizes the importance of rest in the Bible, what makes you think that you don't need it? God's view on rest is clear, so revisit the early chapters of the Bible. After creating the earth and everything on it, God demonstrated the importance of rest by doing just that on the seventh day. God wants us to integrate rest into our daily activity, and He wants us to respect the Sabbath. Appreciate its holiness by spending the appropriate amount of time with Him to recharge your spirit. When you spend less time absorbed in modern devices and more time restoring yourself with appropriate rest, you honor God and become a sharper and more effective servant.

If restlessness makes it hard for you to fall asleep at night, ask God for help. When I can't sleep, I recite a favorite prayer, focusing on the words and allowing my worries and distractions to fade away. As my mind clears, I am able to fall asleep. When you combine mental and spiritual rejuvenation with physical rest, you provide the proper balance God seeks in your life.

Many times, we need to decompress before we rest. I like to break away and find peaceful places of solitude to reflect and seek inspiration. Even during an extremely hectic day, taking some time to clear your mind in a quiet peaceful surrounding can recharge you for the rest of the day.

Personally, I find taking short naps a highly effective means for reenergizing, both physically and mentally. Set the timer on your watch for twenty minutes and then pick a quiet spot. As you wake from a nap or good sleep, say a quick thank you to God and ask Him to provide you with the energy you need for the remainder of the day. Remember, rest is not just about recharging physically. It's also about taking time to revisit your perspective on life. Ask God to provide you with a better perspective on how He wants you to live. Recognize how much easier it is to access Him in quiet and peaceful surroundings. Symbols can bring us peace. Many view the cross, star of David, the sun, the ocean or a creek to be calming. What symbol do you use to embrace your safety net that brings you peace?

I also like to just go outside to walk, or just take deep breaths of fresh air. These moments give me a chance to reflect on my life. God gave you your body to nurture as an earthly vessel for your soul. Don't abuse it. One day, you will have to account for how you cared for it, so be cognizant of what passes through your body, mind and spirit. Appreciate and recognize how much more joyful you are from proper rest. Weekends were not intended to be used to exhaust you, but to refresh you and to respect God's Sabbath day. Recharge with rest! Remember, God devoted his entire seventh day to rest. Shouldn't we, too?

DEEPEN YOUR TRUST IN GOD

- The human battery needs recharging.
- God taught us how to rest by example.
- Don't let your children's activities take over your life.
- Keep the Sabbath.
- Try taking naps to rejuvenate.
- Proper rest builds dynamic action.

CHAPTER 14

TRUST GOD

D o you place at least the same value, focus and reliance on God as you do with your closest friends? If not, why not? You can identify what's missing in your relationship with God by simply appreciating how you view and treat your most treasured human relationships, the people you trust. You should be willing to consistently protect, nurture and strengthen your closest relationships. Trustworthy relationships allow you to enjoy life with individuals who share your integrity.

Our society and the evil one will try to erode your trust in God, especially when things don't go your way. A dear relative of mine was doing everything right in dealing with a desperate ex-husband who started stalking her and her young son. She was terrified. After a few years of sleepless nights and rough encounters, she lay in bed one night exhausted, unable to come up with a better solution. She told me she cried that night and begged God for an answer. The next day she received a call offering a well-paid job in a town a couple of hundred miles away. She was overwhelmed and so thankful for God's intercession. She packed immediately and, with her son by her side, they embarked on their new lives in a safe and stable environment. Trust God.

Another friend of mine had been out of work for three years. Finally, he was hired by a company and had to fly to the West Coast for training. The company paid for the flight and all training expenses. Even with a new job, he was almost destitute after the long period of unemployment. He was ninety days past due on his mortgage, and expected that he would lose his house well before his new job would provide him with enough income for the $1,460 past-due bill. His wife encouraged him to trust God and reminded him that He "is an on-time God." My friend took his seat on the plane, still worried. After takeoff, the man sitting next to him leaned over and said, "Excuse me, but I am trying to figure out why God is telling me to write you a check for $1,460." My friend replied, "I have a new job and I am in training, but I have a final notice due on my mortgage with no means to save my house." The stranger wrote my friend a check for $1,460 and said, "Many years ago, I almost lost my house and I promised God that if I ever paid off my house, I would help someone else facing that challenge. A few months ago, I paid off my mortgage of thirty years." Trust God.

My own "Trust God" moment came on the second day of my daughter's life. My newborn child was rushed into emergency surgery because her diaphragm was not fully developed and her heart shifted to the right side of her chest. Our "moment" lasted two years. In that initial operation, the superb surgical team and fervent community prayers yielded success, getting my daughter out of immediate danger. However, the ordeal left her intestine compromised and led to two years of my wife and me watching our daughter weep in excruciating pain during seemingly endless days and nights of throwing up, cramping, severe pain and doctors' visits, which left even specialists puzzled about the problem. We prayed constantly, asking for God's direction and help in finding us someone who could heal our child. Another painful eruption took us to our local emergency room yet again. That night, my daughter's original surgeon was on duty and insisted on operating immediately. The need was acute. A large part of her intestine had died and was tied in a knot, blocking proper flow, a condition which would have ended her life that night. Instead, God's grace and this amazing doctor's skills saved her life. I would not wish that "Trust God" moment on my worst enemy.

God found another way to communicate to me His tender assurance that He is with all those who experience suffering. My wife's aunt had painted portraits of our children around the time of their second birthdays. When she painted our daughter who'd had surgery, she complained that she was experiencing frustration with the piece. The painting came out with little glowing white marks around our daughter's head. She painted over them, but the spots wouldn't vanish. The piece did look a little off when she finished. The artist was mortified, but she showed the piece to a few people, asking for ways to fix it. When my mother-in-law saw it, she said to leave the painting be. She saw what the rest of us needed to have explained. The little white marks formed an aura surrounding my daughter. They extended to the top of the canvas, plainly representing God and His angels, whose presence was central to the healing of my daughter. We still have that painting, and I still react the same way when I see it. I consider it one of the moments that God communicated with me through a physical, visual sign.

You, too, have similar amazing stories that will deepen your knowledge and love of God when you get better at recognizing God's presence in your daily life. We just need to acknowledge those moments more. A relationship with God starts with the same elements of a friendship that characterize our earthly friendships. Challenge yourself to add these key attributes of human friendship to your time with God: communication, trust and honesty. We bond with each other by sharing life's moments and helping each other in times of need. Your relationship with God should be no different. You will know your relationship with God has improved when you reach the point when you rely on His input for most, if not all, of your significant decisions and actions in a day. With that level of fellowship, you begin to understand what God desires for your life. This bond of trust should be used to shape your actions. Rely on God each day without worry about yesterday or tomorrow. Cast off any anchors holding you back, and hand over your anxieties to God. Seek forgiveness and be sincerely sorry for poor decisions. Be on the lookout for the messages and lessons that strengthen your rapport with God. Allocate more time to read religious and spiritual material. Learn as much as you can about God. When you fall, trust God to catch you. He will.

I remember a time when I was cleaning our house gutters. I was standing on the top step of a six-foot ladder—not a smart move. The area below me was surrounded by trees, several jagged tree stumps, pointed broken branches and an air conditioner. As I started to step down, my feet got tangled and I immediately slipped backwards. My feet flipped up toward the sky and I tumbled headfirst toward the ground. I was completely defenseless. As I felt myself falling, I uttered a simple prayer: "Lord, catch me!"

I should have landed headfirst on a tree stump and broken my neck. Instead, as I was falling I felt an incredible sense of peace overcome my entire body. Miraculously, I landed flat on my back in the only barren spot. I just lay there for a bit. Slowly, I moved around and realized that nothing felt broken or injured. The fall had knocked the wind out of me but everything else seemed fine. As I reflected on what happened, I thanked God for catching me, and I was overwhelmed with how blessed I was to survive that fall. The outcome should have been devastating, but I believe my faith and trust in God saved me that day. Every time I recall that incident, it motivates me to be thankful for God's presence in our lives.

As you work on improving yourself, trust in God. Be on the lookout for His messages and lessons that will enable you to become a better person and strengthen your rapport with Him. You need to put some effort into this. Commit to learning as much as you can about God. Read more religious and spiritual material. Try to identify the inspirations that help you deal with your most difficult dilemmas. Ask God to fill your heart with His love, your mind with His knowledge and your soul with His joy. As your trust in this relationship grows, you will come to understand how much God freely and willingly loves your time together. When you put in the work, the benefits will come.

My hope for you is that the messages I've shared in this book inspire you to open your mind and increase your awareness. I hope the thoughts presented here will provide you with a springboard to explore the many ways God converses with you. If you seek Him, you will find Him. When you find Him, you will know Him. My greatest joy as a writer would be to learn that my book opened you up to the possibilities of a God-centered existence. A satisfying and bountiful life exists for you, and its rewards are beyond all imagination. You don't earn it. You merely have to ask for it and "Trust God."

DEEPEN YOUR TRUST IN GOD

- Make God your best friend.
- God is capable of communicating through physical signs.
- You have to make the moves to deepen your relationship.
- Read more spiritual materials.
- Rely on God more each day.
- Trust God.

ACKNOWLEDGEMENTS

I would like to thank the many inspirations and guidance provided me along this journey. First and foremost, I thank God for His ongoing direction and creative communications, and allowing me to discern them. Thanks to all who helped me, especially John and his team, my wife Theresa, my Mom Rowena, Onycha, Rob, Fr. Steve, Raymond, Jimmy, Kylene, Beth, Fr. Bill, Kenzie, Bob, Rich, Pat, my family, and all the other influences in my life encouraging me to just Trust God.

CPSIA information can be obtained
at www.ICGtesting.com
Printed in the USA
BVHW080003161219
566716BV00002B/10/P